A Child's
American Heritage

Written and Illustrated by

Claudia Blocksom

Troubador Press · San Francisco

Introduction

In the years when America was young, nearly everything people needed was made by their own hands. Cloth, clothing, tools, house, furniture and the food on the table, were all the result of much skill and hard work. The colonists took great pride and care in the things they made. It is no wonder that so many of the everyday items were beautifully crafted, and have lasted so long.

The colonists came from many countries and brought with them different skills and customs. The English, French, Dutch, German, and Spanish all sent major expeditions to settle in the New World. Those who settled the southern colonies brought slaves from Africa to provide half or more of the skilled labor to build the new land. The interaction between these settlers and the first Americans — the Indians — was basic to the new culture. The combination of their ideas and the ingenuity of skillfully using the materials at hand gave rise to an exciting new way of life.

The early American people gave us a heritage of delightful customs and crafts of which we can be proud. The activities in this book will help recreate and enjoy our heritage from the point of view of a young Colonial American.

1 2 3 4 5 6 7 8 9

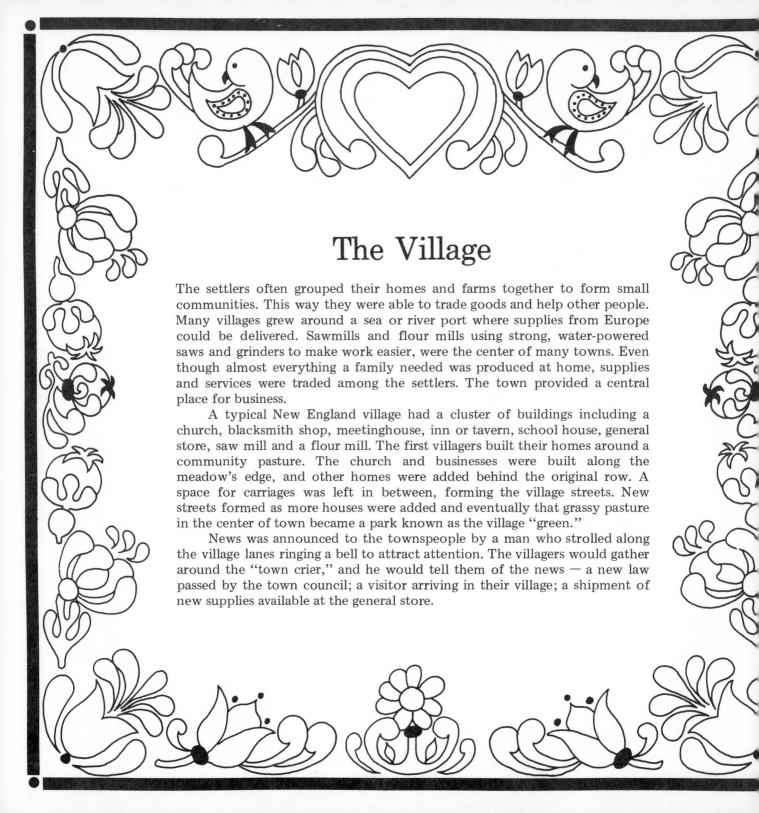

The Village

The settlers often grouped their homes and farms together to form small communities. This way they were able to trade goods and help other people. Many villages grew around a sea or river port where supplies from Europe could be delivered. Sawmills and flour mills using strong, water-powered saws and grinders to make work easier, were the center of many towns. Even though almost everything a family needed was produced at home, supplies and services were traded among the settlers. The town provided a central place for business.

A typical New England village had a cluster of buildings including a church, blacksmith shop, meetinghouse, inn or tavern, school house, general store, saw mill and a flour mill. The first villagers built their homes around a community pasture. The church and businesses were built along the meadow's edge, and other homes were added behind the original row. A space for carriages was left in between, forming the village streets. New streets formed as more houses were added and eventually that grassy pasture in the center of town became a park known as the village "green."

News was announced to the townspeople by a man who strolled along the village lanes ringing a bell to attract attention. The villagers would gather around the "town crier," and he would tell them of the news — a new law passed by the town council; a visitor arriving in their village; a shipment of new supplies available at the general store.

The House

The homes of the Colonial Americans were very simple. The house was usually built of wood, stone or brick. To make the frame of a wooden house, large rough logs were hewn into square timbers. The roofs were thatched or covered with bark at first. Later, wooden shingles would replace the less sturdy coverings. One large room with a sleeping loft was common. Other small side rooms might be added as the family grew.

Often the floor was dirt. The dirt became smooth and hard after months of wear, and the women swept it clean each day. It was the custom in some places to scratch designs into the dirt to decorate the floor like a carpet. At Christmas, holly designs would be etched all around. A birthday greeting might be written on the floor in front of the hearth.

Glass for windows was hard to get and very expensive. Many houses used oiled paper or rows of bottles mortared into wall openings to let in light.

The Dutch and German colonists often built their homes of brick or stone, used for building in their homeland. The Southern colonies were later noted for elaborate country homes, such as George Washington's estate, Mount Vernon.

The picture to color on the next page is a scene of an early American home site.

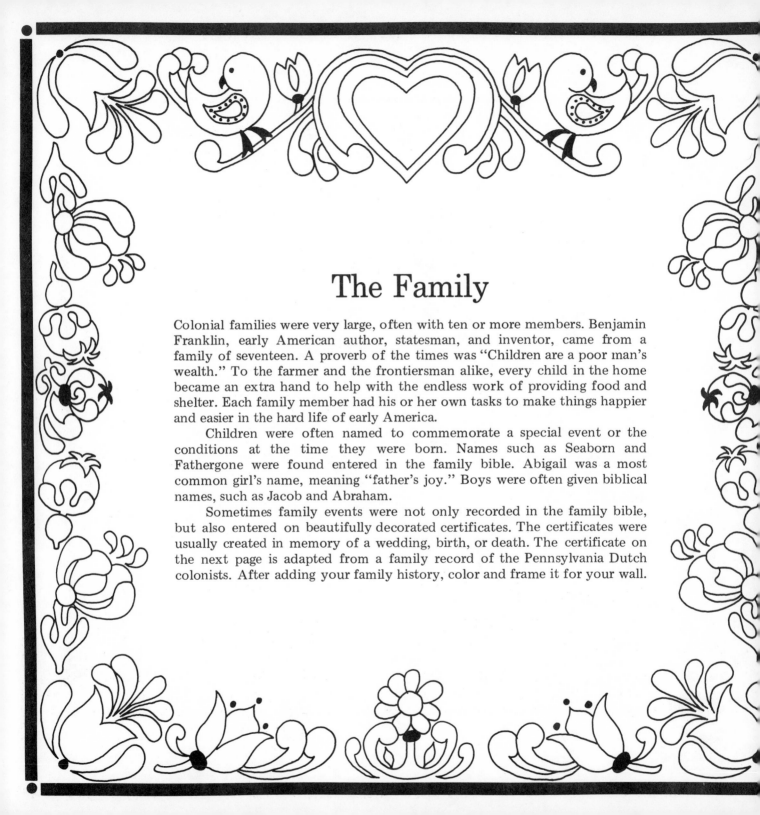

The Family

Colonial families were very large, often with ten or more members. Benjamin Franklin, early American author, statesman, and inventor, came from a family of seventeen. A proverb of the times was "Children are a poor man's wealth." To the farmer and the frontiersman alike, every child in the home became an extra hand to help with the endless work of providing food and shelter. Each family member had his or her own tasks to make things happier and easier in the hard life of early America.

Children were often named to commemorate a special event or the conditions at the time they were born. Names such as Seaborn and Fathergone were found entered in the family bible. Abigail was a most common girl's name, meaning "father's joy." Boys were often given biblical names, such as Jacob and Abraham.

Sometimes family events were not only recorded in the family bible, but also entered on beautifully decorated certificates. The certificates were usually created in memory of a wedding, birth, or death. The certificate on the next page is adapted from a family record of the Pennsylvania Dutch colonists. After adding your family history, color and frame it for your wall.

My Family Tree

child's name

date of birth

place of birth

mother's name

father's name

date and place of birth

date and place of birth

grandmother

grandmother

grandfather

grandfather

Sisters' names

Brothers' names

The Kitchen

The big stone fireplace in early American homes was the center of family life. It served as the stove, the heater, and a source of light after sunset. The women did most of the cooking in huge iron kettles and skillets over the open fire. A small opening beside the main fireplace was used for baking, or sometimes brick ovens were built outside. A sheet iron box with one open side, called a roasting oven, was placed on the hearth for cooking meats. It wasn't until the 1800's that a cook stove separate from the fireplace was introduced.

Most colonists provided all of their own food. A typical family would have a cow, ducks, and chickens, gardens of vegetables and herbs, as well as a fruit orchard. Everyone, down to the youngest child, worked to feed and tend the vital stock.

The early American homemaker created many delicious new ways of preparing the foods available in the new land. Many of those recipes have been handed down through the generations. With slight variations for the foods available today, these recipes can be prepared and enjoyed by your family.

Johnny Cakes:

Johnny cake is a biscuit-style cake made from cornmeal. The cake had many names: "Journey Cake", since it was often included in travelers' food supplies; "Hoe Cake", since it was baked before the fire on a flat metal tool with a long handle; "Shawnee Cake", since the original recipe was learned from the Indians.

There are many variations of the recipe. Here is one you can enjoy. Try using honey in place of molasses if you'd prefer, or make 3-4 small cakes instead of one large one!

Johnny Cakes ~

2 cups milk
6 cups cornmeal
1 cup flour

1 teaspoon salt
½ cup molasses

Scald milk (heat until tiny bubbles form around pot.) Carefully add all of the other ingredients. Batter will be stiff. Pour onto cookie sheet. Bake at 350°, until golden brown.

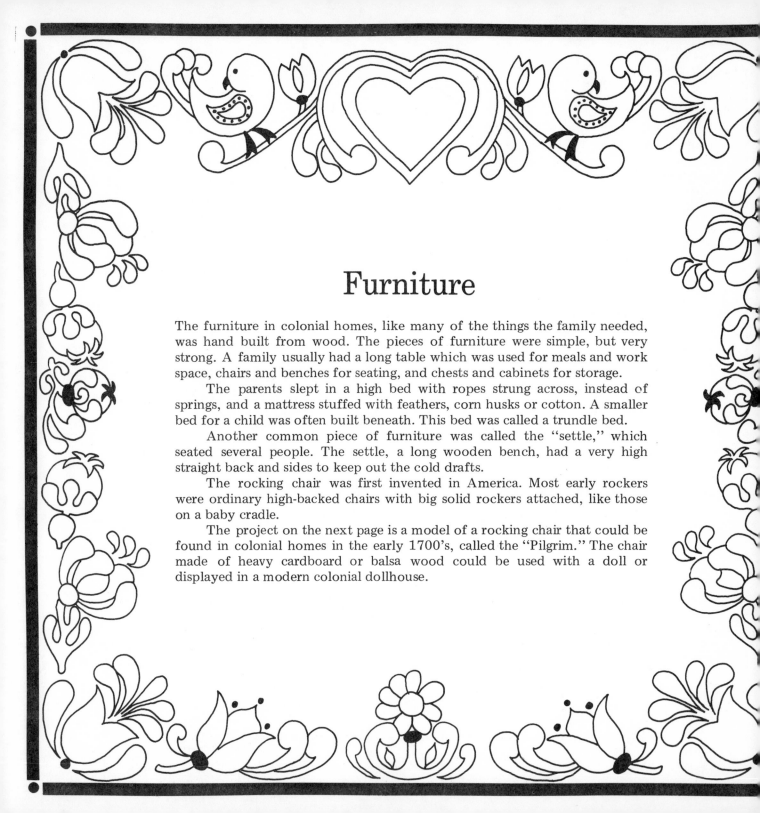

Furniture

The furniture in colonial homes, like many of the things the family needed, was hand built from wood. The pieces of furniture were simple, but very strong. A family usually had a long table which was used for meals and work space, chairs and benches for seating, and chests and cabinets for storage.

The parents slept in a high bed with ropes strung across, instead of springs, and a mattress stuffed with feathers, corn husks or cotton. A smaller bed for a child was often built beneath. This bed was called a trundle bed.

Another common piece of furniture was called the "settle," which seated several people. The settle, a long wooden bench, had a very high straight back and sides to keep out the cold drafts.

The rocking chair was first invented in America. Most early rockers were ordinary high-backed chairs with big solid rockers attached, like those on a baby cradle.

The project on the next page is a model of a rocking chair that could be found in colonial homes in the early 1700's, called the "Pilgrim." The chair made of heavy cardboard or balsa wood could be used with a doll or displayed in a modern colonial dollhouse.

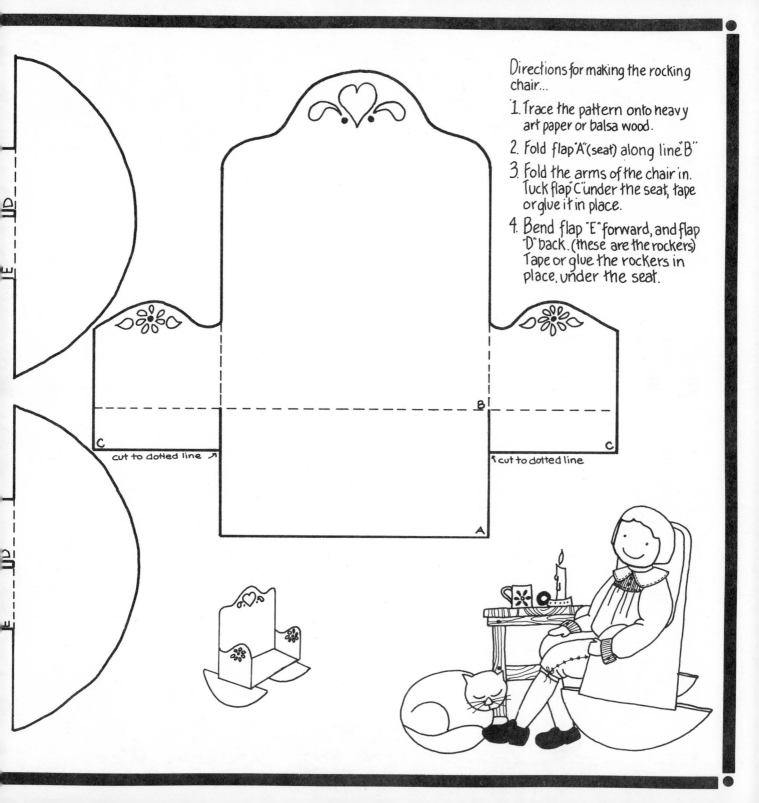

Directions for making the rocking chair...

1. Trace the pattern onto heavy art paper or balsa wood.

2. Fold flap "A" (seat) along line "B"

3. Fold the arms of the chair in. Tuck flap "C" under the seat, tape or glue it in place.

4. Bend flap "E" forward, and flap "D" back. (these are the rockers) Tape or glue the rockers in place, under the seat.

cut to dotted line

cut to dotted line

Clothing

Fashion in early America was set by the styles in Europe, but was modified slightly to suit the activities of the new land. The styles also varied from colony to colony. The Quakers, for example, wore simple styles in drab colors, while the Southern colonists dressed in lively bright fashions from France.

Generally, the clothes were sturdy and fashioned for long wear. Sewing was done at home by hand, with each garment requiring hours of painstaking work. The wardrobes of the early Americans were limited to one or two sets of everyday clothes and one Sunday outfit.

Young boys and girls were dressed alike in long loose gowns until age six. Older girls dressed as their mothers, with shorter skirts. Boys wore smock-style shirts tucked into loose knee-length pants.

The costumes shown on the next page are examples of early American dress. Perhaps you could modify your or your family's clothes and recreate these traditional styles to wear to an American heritage celebration.

The gentleman is dressed in Quaker fashion. He is wearing a wide-brimmed black felt hat turned up in front. His waistcoat and knee breeches are made of dark gray cloth. The buttons are covered in the same cloth. A white scarf is knotted at his neck. Under the fitted gray vest, he would wear a simple collarless white shirt. He also would wear gray wool stockings and simple black leather shoes.

The colonial lady wears a tight little cotton cap to cover her hair. The long dress has loose sleeves that are turned back at her elbows. You can see the sleeves of a chemise (underdress). A full shoulder wrap, called a "fichu", is tied at the waist. A long white apron was worn to protect the dress. Transparent, mesh-like, fingerless gloves were in fashion to cover the lower arms. Ladies usually wore simple black slippers.

Quilting

The Patchwork quilt originated in America. Comforters, brought for bedding on the long voyage from Europe and used in the colonists' first homes, soon became worn. When mending them, the women added bits of cloth as patches. As new blankets were needed, scraps of old clothing and linen were pieced together. Soon the women were planning patterns, shapes, and designs to create beautiful patchwork quilts.

The quilts were stuffed with wool, cotton, or feathers. Straw, cornhusks, or milkweed down were used when other materials for warmth were not available.

The patchwork quilts sewn by the early American women became cherished family possessions. The "quilting bee," where women shared the long task of stitching the quilt, became a joyful social event. The patterns created have been passed down the generations and many people use these designs today. The pattern used in the project on the next page is called "Shoo-Fly."

How to make a
quilted patchwork
potholder...

1. Cut pieces of fabric in
the shapes shown.
(cut them about ¼ inch
larger for seams)

2. Sew all of the pieces
together to match the
pattern.

3. Cut one piece of heavy
fabric, the same size as
the finished patchwork
(this will be the back).

4. For protection, put a
layer of padding between
the two pieces.

5. Bind the edges of the
potholder with seam
binding tape, or a long
strip of folded fabric.

6. To keep all layers together,
use tiny stitches, and
quilt along the lines
shown.

7. Sew a ring or loop of fabric
to one corner, if you
want to hang the
pot holder.

sew all of
the patches
together...

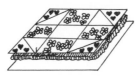

place patchwork,
on top of padding.
then on backing.

bind all three
layers together .
around edge.

use tiny quilting
stitches, through
all layers.

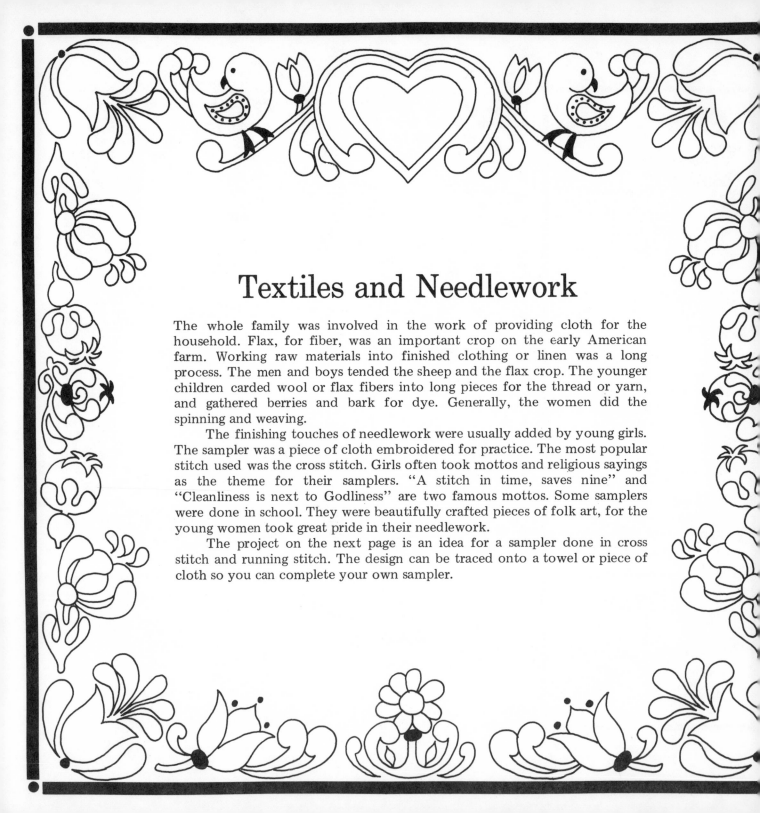

Textiles and Needlework

The whole family was involved in the work of providing cloth for the household. Flax, for fiber, was an important crop on the early American farm. Working raw materials into finished clothing or linen was a long process. The men and boys tended the sheep and the flax crop. The younger children carded wool or flax fibers into long pieces for the thread or yarn, and gathered berries and bark for dye. Generally, the women did the spinning and weaving.

The finishing touches of needlework were usually added by young girls. The sampler was a piece of cloth embroidered for practice. The most popular stitch used was the cross stitch. Girls often took mottos and religious sayings as the theme for their samplers. "A stitch in time, saves nine" and "Cleanliness is next to Godliness" are two famous mottos. Some samplers were done in school. They were beautifully crafted pieces of folk art, for the young women took great pride in their needlework.

The project on the next page is an idea for a sampler done in cross stitch and running stitch. The design can be traced onto a towel or piece of cloth so you can complete your own sampler.

When you feel all steamed up
Remember the tea kettle,
It is always up to its neck
in hot water,
And still it sings.

Running Stitch:

The words of the sampler are done using a line of running stitches. Catch only a few threads of fabric between stitches.

Cross Stitch:

1.

2

The rest of this sampler is done in cross stitch. Make a row of diagonal stitches, then complete the cross by working back in the other direction.

Flowers and Herbs

All early Americans lived in close contact with their natural environment. They studied and experimented with the wild plants surrounding their homes, and found many household uses for them: herbs for seasoning, drinks, and medicine; flowers for scents and decoration.

The clever colonial homemakers soon had long lists of folk cures for common ailments. They brewed teas from herbs and blended salves and ointment from wild growing ingredients. The most popular wild plants soon became an essential and carefully cultivated part of the family garden.

During the Revolutionary War, and even before because of the hated tax, patriotic Americans gave up imported teas. In place of the beloved English imported tea, the teapots steamed with brews from blackberry leaves, young currant leaves, or sage blossoms.

Colonial ladies even blended their own perfumes and scents for soaps and cosmetics. They used nature's own beautiful fragrances to give harsh homemade soaps a more delicate and appealing smell. They brewed mixtures of flower buds and petals into lovely natural perfumes. The next page has a colonial recipe for rose water perfume and instructions for making a naturally scented pillow.

Rose Water

Pick one and a half pounds of rose petals. Put one or two cups of petals in a pot, add a very small amount of water. Cook over slow heat for thirty minutes. Strain; return liquid to the pot; add more petals; only add more water if necessary to keep from burning. Repeat this process until all petals are used. Strain the liquid through cheesecloth into jars. Keep tightly sealed, wait three days before using.

Scented Pillows

Allow picked rose petals to dry in the sun on a screen. To the well-dried petals, add a small amount of dried sweet basil, dried mint leaves, and some ground cloves. Mix well, and use to stuff small pillows. The pillows may scent drawers and closets. Folklore says that these pillows will induce peaceful sleep and fragrant dreams!

Toys

Colonial children were kept busy doing their share of house and farm work. When the chores were done there was time for play.

The most common toys found in the toy shops were dolls. At first, the dolls were sent to America to illustrate the fashion trends of Europe. Toy shops were few, and the fancy goods from France and England were very expensive, so American children usually made their own toys.

Girls would sew dolls from scraps of cloth. Boys would whittle clever playthings from wood. A highly desired possession for a boy was his jackknife.

Many of the toys were enjoyed by the whole family. Sunday was the day when the entire family rested and spent the day together. Toys were brought out to amuse everyone. The name "Sunday Toy" was given to the many clever objects used for family entertainment.

The simple toy from the early 1800's on the next page can be made, perhaps with the help of an adult, from lightweight wood.

14"

5"

8"

(paper fasteners pushed through drilled holes)

The Happy Woodsmen

1. Use balsawood, or heavy art-board.

2. Cut out two woodsman figures. Their axes are cut as part of their bodies, from the same piece.

3. Cut out the two handles.

4. Cut out a tree stump shape.

5. Paint the figures and stump with acrylic or enamel paint.

6. Glue the stump on to the center of one of the handles.

7. Drill two holes in each figure (approx ⅛") and two holes in each handle as shown.

8. Use paper fasteners to hold the figures on to the handles.

Push and pull the handles ... the men rock back and forth and chop the tree!

Games

The games that colonial children played were handed down from one child to another, year after year. Many had their beginnings in religious celebrations. Some had songs, verses, or morals.

One game, we would call "pitching pennies," was known as "chuck-farthing." Imagine a group of children tossing coins into a box or board with a hole for a target (like a bean bag toss). Chuck-farthing had a rhyme to tell you how to play, as well as a moral.

> *As you value your pence,*
> *   at the hole take your aim*
> *Chuck all safely in,*
> *   and you'll win the game.*
>
> *Chuck-farthing like trade,*
> *   requires great care,*
> *The more you observe,*
> *   the better you'll fare.*

The game on the next page was for outdoor play at harvest time. The adults set up the maze with bales of hay, branches or bundles of straw out in the field. The children found their way to the prizes in the center while the parents enjoyed a harvest-time feast.

The maze shown can be laid out on a playground using ropes, branches, or even drawn with chalk. A group or class could have a race against time and prizes could be placed in the center of the maze. You can also use the maze as a puzzle page and to find your way to the center with your finger or a pencil.

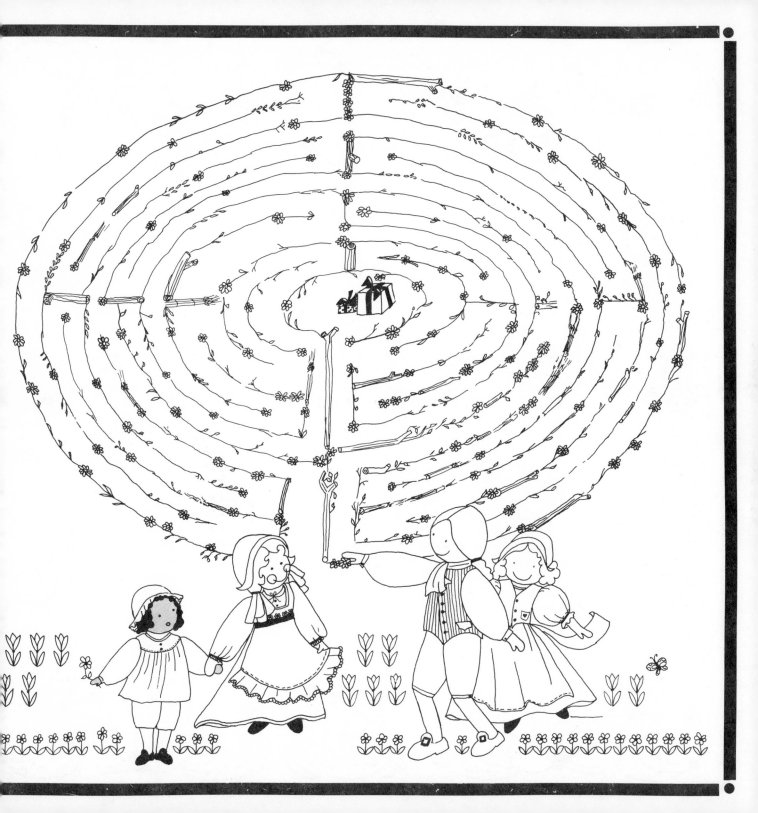

Music

Music was an important part of life in early America. Each group of people had its traditional folk music from Europe.

Many colonists were religious people and voiced their faith in beautiful hymns. On Sunday mornings the air would be filled with the singing voices of church-goers.

Slaves brought their musical tradition to America from all parts of Africa. With a major effect on much of our American music, this music told of everyday life in a sometimes happy, often soulful and tragic style. The banjo, often used as accompaniment, was introduced to America by the slaves and has become a common instrument in American music.

Those that were wealthy participated in a style of music set by fashion in Europe. The women and girls played the harpsichord or spinet, keyboard instruments similar to the piano of today. The boys were taught the violin.

As time passed, new songs expressing life in the new land were created. Much of the folk music at this time told of the struggles in the new land and of young America's path to freedom. It helps us remember the people, events and spirit that led to the forming of the United States as we know it.

The next page has a song and music from America's colonial period that you might enjoy singing and playing today.

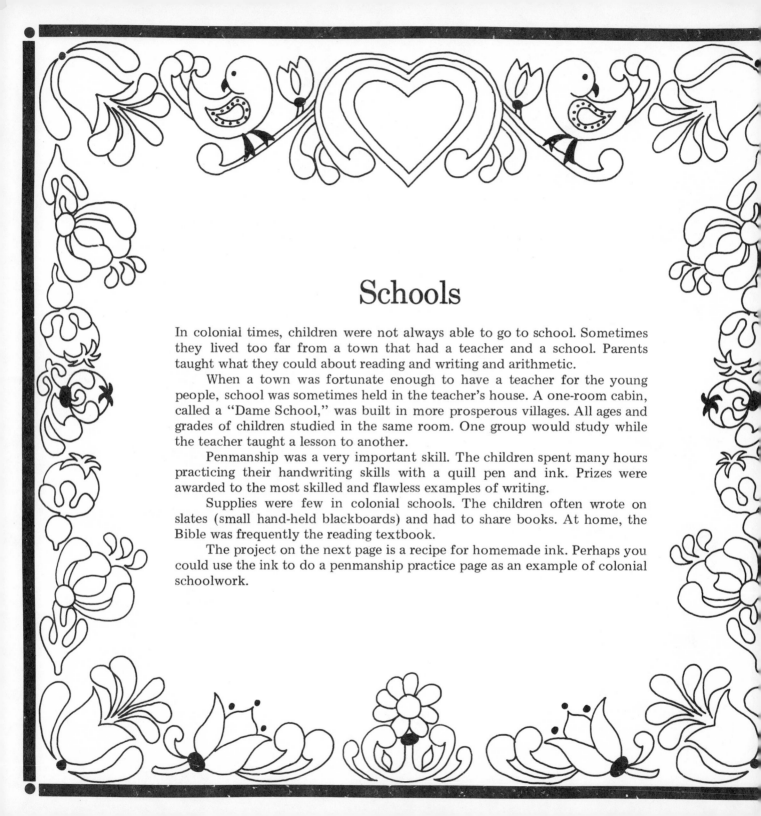

Schools

In colonial times, children were not always able to go to school. Sometimes they lived too far from a town that had a teacher and a school. Parents taught what they could about reading and writing and arithmetic.

When a town was fortunate enough to have a teacher for the young people, school was sometimes held in the teacher's house. A one-room cabin, called a "Dame School," was built in more prosperous villages. All ages and grades of children studied in the same room. One group would study while the teacher taught a lesson to another.

Penmanship was a very important skill. The children spent many hours practicing their handwriting skills with a quill pen and ink. Prizes were awarded to the most skilled and flawless examples of writing.

Supplies were few in colonial schools. The children often wrote on slates (small hand-held blackboards) and had to share books. At home, the Bible was frequently the reading textbook.

The project on the next page is a recipe for homemade ink. Perhaps you could use the ink to do a penmanship practice page as an example of colonial schoolwork.

Home-made Ink

crush several empty walnut shells into very small pieces...

in a saucepan, cover the shells with boiling water...

simmer until the liquid is very dark brown...

add some salt and vinegar, (this will "set" the color.)

strain the ink through a piece of cheesecloth into a jar.

You can use this ink in any pen that dips or fills with ink.

Folktale

This is a folk tale which came to America with the slaves who were brought to work on the southern plantations. This version of the story was found on St. Helena Island, South Carolina.

Once upon a time, on a quiet little farm, there lived a mule named Sam. Sam worked hard all week plowing and hauling for his owner. On Sunday, after taking the family wagon to church, Sam rested in a big green grassy meadow.

One Sunday afternoon the farmer had to go back into town to get some medicine for his little daughter. He sent his son out to put the saddle on Sam. The boy went out to the barn.

"Move over, Sam!" he said as he reached for the saddle.

"For gosh sake, have I got to work on Sunday?" complained Sam.

The astonished boy dropped the saddle and ran out of the barn and into the farmhouse.

"Sam doesn't want to work on Sunday. He told me so!" cried the son.

The farmer was angered by his son telling such a silly tale and stormed out to saddle the mule himself.

"Move over, Sam," he said impatiently.

"Hmmmm, you say, 'Move over, Sam,' but you don't even bring me anything nice to eat!" said Sam.

The farmer dropped the saddle and ran outside.

"I never heard a mule talk before!" he exclaimed.

"Neither did I," added the dog that had followed him into the barn.

The farmer ran even faster into the house after hearing that!

"The mule talked!" panted the man to his wife.

"What!" she exclaimed.

"I said, 'I never heard a mule talk before' and then the dog said 'Me neither.' "

"Ridiculous!" said the wife.

Just then the cat ran in, hearing all the excitement.

"That is ridiculous," said the cat. "Everyone knows mules and dogs can not talk . . ."

THE END

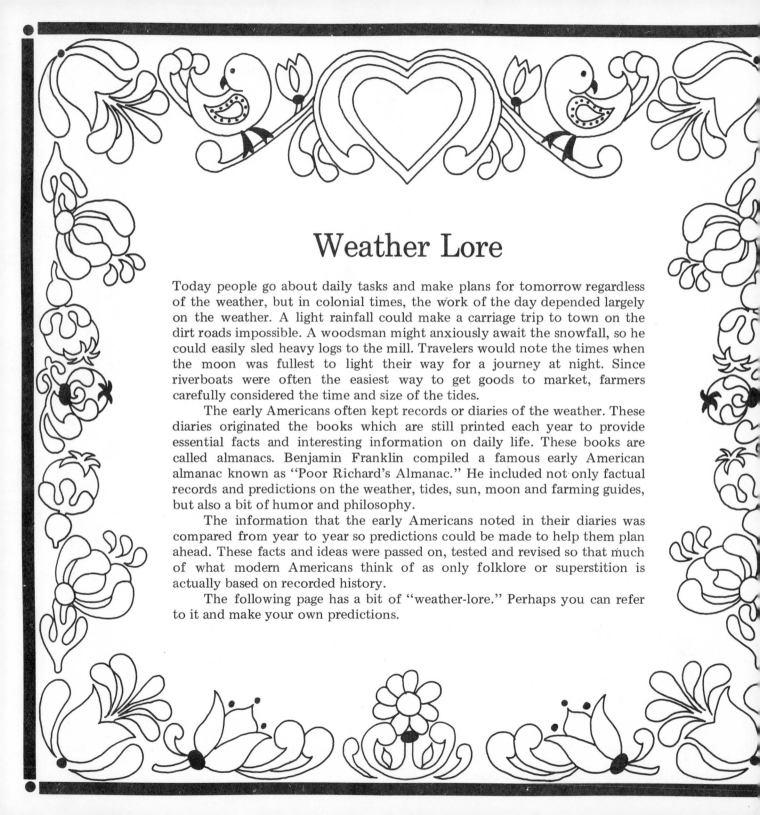

Weather Lore

Today people go about daily tasks and make plans for tomorrow regardless of the weather, but in colonial times, the work of the day depended largely on the weather. A light rainfall could make a carriage trip to town on the dirt roads impossible. A woodsman might anxiously await the snowfall, so he could easily sled heavy logs to the mill. Travelers would note the times when the moon was fullest to light their way for a journey at night. Since riverboats were often the easiest way to get goods to market, farmers carefully considered the time and size of the tides.

The early Americans often kept records or diaries of the weather. These diaries originated the books which are still printed each year to provide essential facts and interesting information on daily life. These books are called almanacs. Benjamin Franklin compiled a famous early American almanac known as "Poor Richard's Almanac." He included not only factual records and predictions on the weather, tides, sun, moon and farming guides, but also a bit of humor and philosophy.

The information that the early Americans noted in their diaries was compared from year to year so predictions could be made to help them plan ahead. These facts and ideas were passed on, tested and revised so that much of what modern Americans think of as only folklore or superstition is actually based on recorded history.

The following page has a bit of "weather-lore." Perhaps you can refer to it and make your own predictions.

Weather-Lore

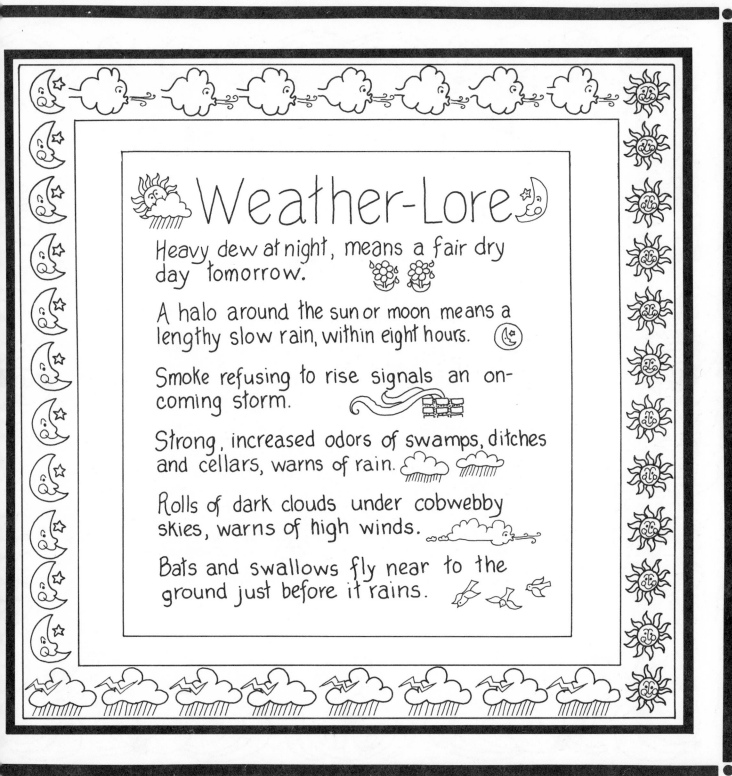

Heavy dew at night, means a fair dry day tomorrow.

A halo around the sun or moon means a lengthy slow rain, within eight hours.

Smoke refusing to rise signals an on-coming storm.

Strong, increased odors of swamps, ditches and cellars, warns of rain.

Rolls of dark clouds under cobwebby skies, warns of high winds.

Bats and swallows fly near to the ground just before it rains.

Indians

The native Americans, named Indians by the explorers who thought they had found a western route to India, were from a culture that has had a lasting influence on American heritage. Their way of life was well suited to their natural surroundings. The Indians made the best use of the materials at hand, without upsetting the balance of nature.

The colonists learned many things from the American Indians to make a good life in the new land. The Indians showed them how to get sap from the maple tree. From the sap, sugar and syrup were made. Indians also showed the colonists how to plant squash and pumpkin successfully.

One of the more important contributions of Indian life to the settlers was the plant called maize, or corn. The new Americans found many uses for the plant they saw growing in the villages of the first Americans. The Indians used the corn plant in many clever ways. The ear of corn was eaten fresh or dried and ground into meal. The husks, or leaves that surround the ear, were braided into ropes and mats. Children made dolls from corn husks. The settlers tied the husks into brooms and used husks as mattress stuffing.

The next page has a project using corn husks. You can prepare the corn for a meal, and use the husks from the ears of corn to make the husk rope.

Making a corn husk rope...

I. Prepare the corn husks...
A. Use the husks from 12 ears of corn.
B. Place the husks between 2 sheets of paper. Allow them to dry for two weeks.
C. The day before use, sprinkle the husks with water and flatten. Carefully place them in a large plastic bag, close it tightly until ready to use.
D. Spread the husks flat on a damp towel. Keep them damp as you work.

II. Start the rope...
A. Trim all pieces to an even length, 6-8 inches long.
B. Cut three husks with an angle cut; trim one, 1 inch shorter than the first, the other, 1 inch shorter than that.
C. Roll the three husks into long narrow strips.
D. Fasten the three husks at the straight end with carpet thread.
E. Braid the husks into a rope.
F. To add husks, slip a rolled husk into the short strand, and continue to braid, adding husks until your rope is as long as you'd like.

① 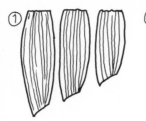 trim the first husks with an angle cut...

②  roll each into a narrow strip...

③  bind together with thread...

④  fasten to a steady hook to hold it while braiding

⑤ 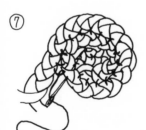 tuck another rolled husk into strand as it gets short...

⑥  continue, adding more husks and braiding... bind the ends with thread.

⑦  If you make a rope 6 ft. long, you can coil it into an 8 in. mat by stitching the coil together with carpet thread. It would make an excellent hot-mat for your table!

The Pennsylvania Dutch

The colonists known as the Pennsylvania Dutch came from the Rhineland and settled in America in the 1700's. The Pennsylvania Dutch included a variety of religious groups and some specially talented craftsmen and their families. They created a new way of life and a style of art that was different from all other colonies.

The Pennsylvania Dutch were noted for their sturdy, well-kept houses, and massive wood, or wood and stone, barns with oak beams and rafters in the European tradition. They are also remembered for the folk art they created. The tools, furniture, pottery, and textiles they made were not only sturdy and useful, but beautifully decorated with flower and bird motifs. The painted and carved decorations were based on traditional symbols from their homeland, as well as on their new daily life. The art and life style they originated has left a lasting memory of happy, hard-working, religious people who loved their homes and had pride in their work.

Here are just a few examples of the many traditional symbols used to decorate dishes, furniture, boxes, tools, and particularly the barns. You can trace them to decorate a project of your own. You could paint an old chair, a tin bucket, or even a lunch box.

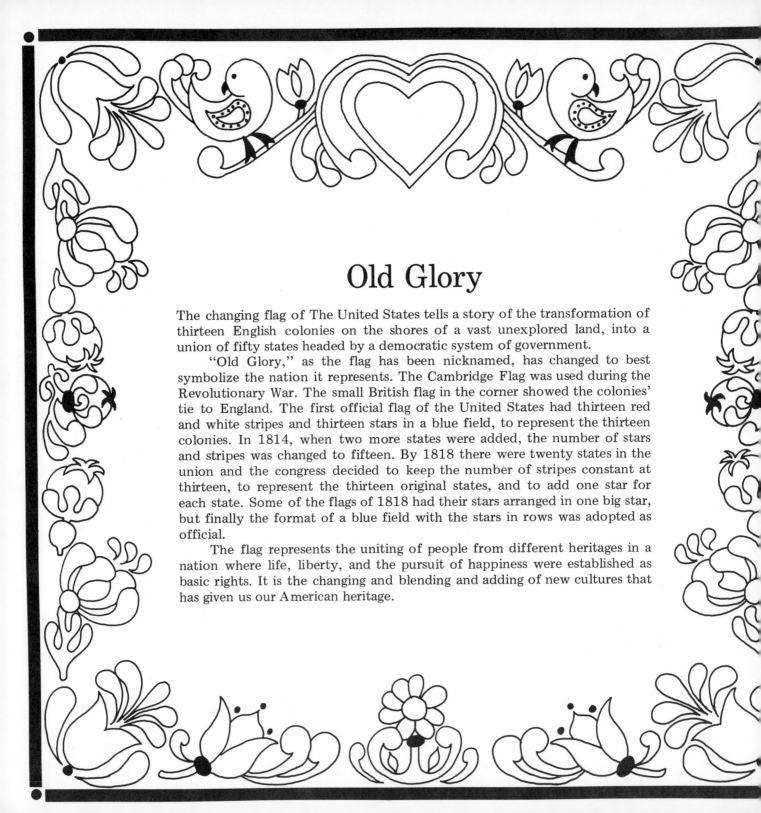

Old Glory

The changing flag of The United States tells a story of the transformation of thirteen English colonies on the shores of a vast unexplored land, into a union of fifty states headed by a democratic system of government.

"Old Glory," as the flag has been nicknamed, has changed to best symbolize the nation it represents. The Cambridge Flag was used during the Revolutionary War. The small British flag in the corner showed the colonies' tie to England. The first official flag of the United States had thirteen red and white stripes and thirteen stars in a blue field, to represent the thirteen colonies. In 1814, when two more states were added, the number of stars and stripes was changed to fifteen. By 1818 there were twenty states in the union and the congress decided to keep the number of stripes constant at thirteen, to represent the thirteen original states, and to add one star for each state. Some of the flags of 1818 had their stars arranged in one big star, but finally the format of a blue field with the stars in rows was adopted as official.

The flag represents the uniting of people from different heritages in a nation where life, liberty, and the pursuit of happiness were established as basic rights. It is the changing and blending and adding of new cultures that has given us our American heritage.

Cambridge Flag 1775

First United States Flag 1777

Star Spangled Banner 1814

Thirteen Stripe Flag 1818

Great Star Flag 1818

The Flag of The United States 1975

MORE ENTERTAINING BOOKS FROM TROUBADOR PRESS

ACTIVITY BOOKS

Auto Racing Color and Story	$2.00
Beasties Color Book	2.00
Dinosaur Color Book	2.00
Fat Cat Coloring and Limerick Book	2.00
Fifty Years of Cars — Models to Make	2.00
Geometric Playthings — Cut and Build	2.00
Kachina Dolls Cut Outs	2.00
Los Angeles Scenes	2.00
Love Bug Color and Limerick Book	2.00
Monster Gallery Color and Story Book	2.00
New York Scenes	2.00
North American Birdlife Coloring Album	2.00
North American Sealife Coloring Album	2.00
North American Wildflowers Coloring Album	2.00
North American Wildlife Coloring Album	2.00
New Testament Color and Story Book	2.00
Old Testament Color and Story Book	2.00
Paper Airplanes — Color Fold and Fly	2.00
Paper Movie Machines — Ready to Make	2.00
San Francisco Scenes	2.00
Science Fiction Anthology — Color and Story	2.00
Zodiac Color Book	2.00

FAT CAT FUN BOOKS

A Child's American Heritage	1.50
Fat Cat's Cookbook	1.50
Fat Cat's Craftbook	1.50
It's Your World Ecology Book	1.50
Meanings of Christmas	1.50
Nature Crafts and Projects	1.50
Once Upon A Time	1.50
Small World Cookbook	1.50

TROUBADOR SPECIALS

International Folk Crafts	$1.50
Monster Movie Game	2.00
Nature's Pets	1.50
Optricks	1.50
Optricks II	1.50
Think Metrics	1.50

GIFT EDITIONS

Aphrodisiac Cookery (hb)	4.95
The Bath Book (hb)	5.95
The Bath Book (pb)	2.95
The Scrimshander (pb)	6.95
Sprouting Cookbook (hb)	5.95
Sprouting Cookbook (pb)	3.95
Yogurt Cookbook (pb)	3.95

PUZZLEBOOKS

Maze Craze	1.50
Maze Craze II	1.50
Maze Craze III	1.50
Puzzlers	1.50

TROUBADOR PRESS · 126 FOLSOM STREET · SAN FRANCISCO, CA 94105